GREAT WESTERN STEAM at Swindon Works

GREAT WESTERN STEAM AT SWINDON WORKS

BRIAN MORRISON

D. BRADFORD BARTON LIMITED

Frontispiece: 'City' Class 4-4-0 No.3440 *City of Truro* at Swindon after working the Railway Correspondence & Travel Society's 'Moonraker' special train from Paddington in August 1957. Built in 1903 to Churchward's design, this engine is said to have attained a speed of over 100mph whilst hauling an Ocean Liner Express down Wellington bank in 1904. On withdrawal in 1931 she was transferred to York Museum for preservation and in 1957 after complete overhaul at Swindon Works was returned to traffic for hauling enthusiasts' specials. *City of Truro* was also used on the Didcot, Newbury and Southampton line on normal traffic and is now in Swindon Museum.

© copyright D. Bradford Barton Ltd 1975   ISBN 0 85153 158 X

printed in Great Britain by Chapel River Press (IPC Printers), Andover for the publishers

D. BRADFORD BARTON LTD · Trethellan House · Truro · Cornwall · England

introduction

During the 1950's I set myself the task of obtaining a photographic record of every locomotive class and sub-class then at work upon British Railways. To complete the Southern it was necessary to travel from Kent, where I live, to North Cornwall; for completion of both Eastern and Midland, visits to Scotland were required, in addition to sheds at such places as Accrington, Burton, Carnforth, Doncaster and the like, almost through the alphabet. The Western Region, however, was a different story. Although its variety of locomotion stretched from London into Cheshire, South Wales and the West Country, all of it—at one time or another—seemed to appear at Swindon Works either for overhaul or destined for scrapping. Thus the gamut of what had become the Western Region, ranging from the locomotives of Dean, Churchward, Collett and Hawksworth to those of the small lines absorbed by the GWR such as the Cardiff Railway, Burry Port & Gwendraeth Valley, Midland & South Western Junction, Cambrian, Rhymney and Taff Vale, plus a number of the BR Standard types that were then prevalent, could be recorded by visits to the Works over a period of time. Swindon was a place that was always interesting no matter how many visits were made, and where one began finally to expect the unexpected. One might see a Bulleid Pacific or *Duke of Gloucester* at work on the Test Plant; a crash-damaged Class 9F for repair; withdrawn *City of Truro* completely overhauled for further service; or a Vale of Rheidol locomotive on special 1ft 11½in gauge track amid the mighty 'Kings' and 'Castles'. The sadness one felt in observing the older engines being cut up was offset by seeing others still being constructed and it was always pleasant to observe a class that appeared to be in for scrapping but which in fact emerged some little time later after a complete overhaul and repaint, good for a number of years further active service.

In compiling this volume, an attempt has been made to include as many of the locomotive types to be seen at Swindon in the 1950's as possible; included also are examples of the places within the Works where they could be seen, such as the Erecting Shop, Works Yards, Cutting-Up Shop, the Triangle plus one or two in the Running Shed itself.

1400 Class 0-4-2T No.1415 in the Works Yard after a complete overhaul and repaint. These locomotives were designed by Collett in 1932 for light branch line use and were fitted for push and pull working. The class was originally designated 4800 and 75 were built, plus another 20 without auto fitting that were designated as 5800s.

'Modified Hall' Class No. 7918 *Rhose Wood Hall* outside the Works in February 1955 after overhaul. This class was a 1944 Hawksworth development of the original Collett class of 1924, as depicted on page 84. The 71 engines of the class were built with 'one piece' main frames and plate framed bogie plus a larger superheater.

'County' Class No. 1000 *County of Middlesex* outside the Works minus tender in November 1955, newly painted in green livery. These locomotives were Hawksworth's only large design, 30 being built between 1945 and 1947. The large double chimney was replaced in 1958.

1600 Class 0-6-0PT No. 1660 under construction in the Erecting Shop in February 1955. These Hawksworth-designed pannier tanks were for light branch work and shunting, and eventually numbered seventy.

Ex-Taff Vale Railway 'A' Class 0-6-2T No.397 outside the Works on a dull August day in 1957. The class was designed by Cameron in 1914 and rebuilt by the GWR in 1924 with a superheated taper boiler. No.397 is shown with rounded side tanks.

Another Taff Vale 'A' Class, with square side tanks. No. 383, as with the rest of the class, was greatly improved as to steaming qualities by the GWR re-boilering. There were 58 in the class and a few survived until as late as 1957.

Ex-Burry Port and Gwendraeth Valley Railway 0-6-0T No. 2166 on the scrap road outside the Cutting-up Shop, June 1955. This was an original and un-modified Hudswell Clarke design, circa 1912.

Ex-Cardiff Railway 0-6-0PT No. 684 in the Works Yard in October 1954. These locomoti[ves] were a Hope and Hudswell Clarke design of 1920 and were re-boilered by the GWR a[nd] fitted with pannier tanks.

Ex-Rhymney Railway 'R1' Class 0-6-2T No. 36, having been brought in dead from So[uth] Wales as part of a freight train, awaits moving from Swindon shed to the Works [for] breaking up. This class was a Hurry Riches development of 1921 from the original 1[?] 'R' Class.

Ex-Cambrian Railway 0-6-0 No. 849, minus tender, outside the Cutting-up Shop on the 'Dump' in October 1954. This class was designed by Jones in 1903 and re-boilered by the GWR from 1924 onwards.

Ex-Burry Port and Gwendraeth Valley Railway 0-6-0T No. 2165, introduced in 1912 Hudswell Clarke & Co of Leeds but rebuilt by the GWR, being reduced to scrap insi the Cutting-up Shop, April 1955.

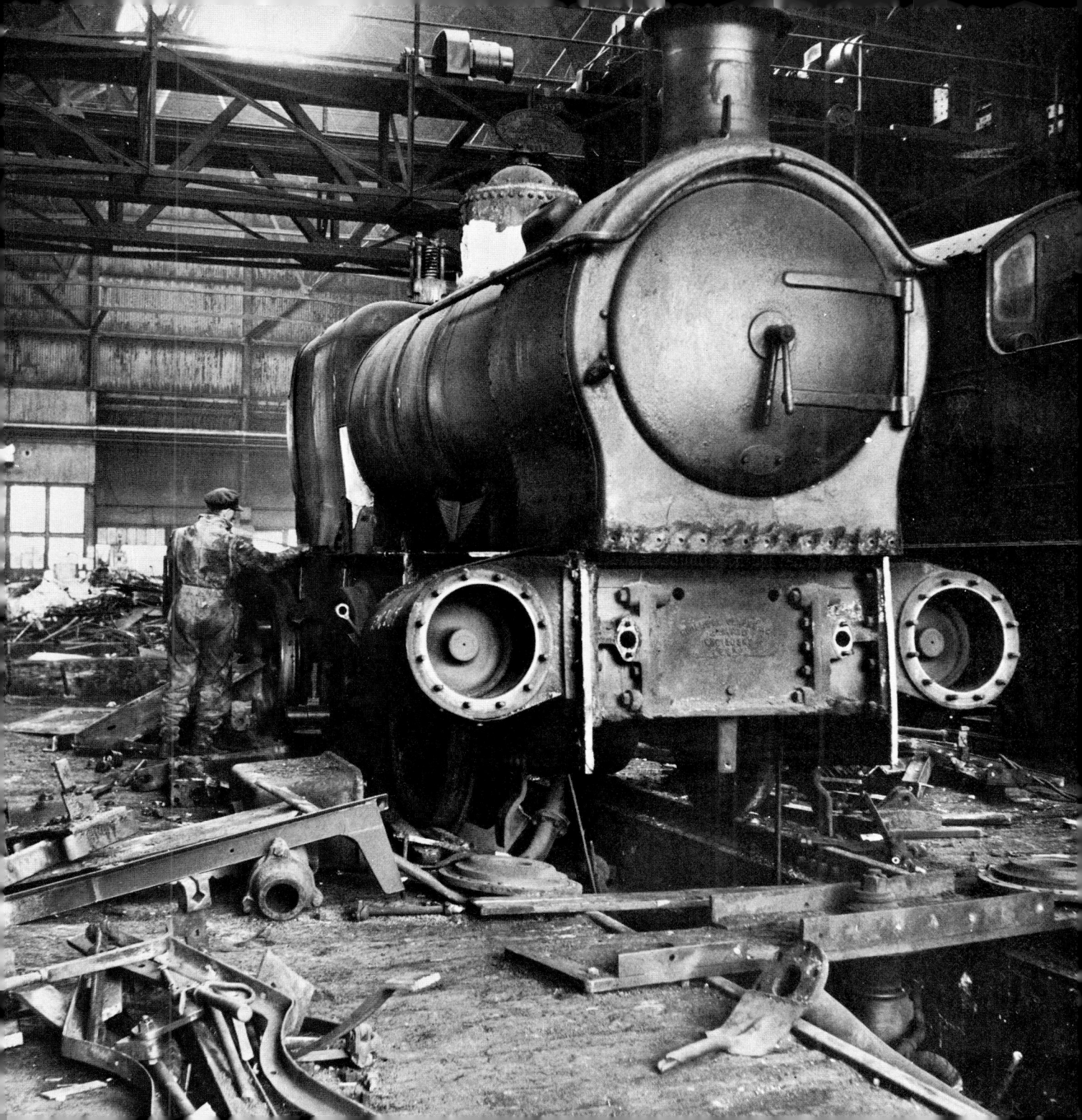

R.O.D. Class 2-8-0 No. 3023 outside the Works on the 'Triangle' in November 1955. After World War I the G W R acquired over 100 of these engines and the best fifty were retained in service. Originally a Robinson design for the Great Central Railway, hundreds were built for the Railway Operating Division for use overseas but here the Great Western influence shows itself with chimney and various other fittings. All but five of the class lasted until after World War II and the advent of Nationalisation.

4500 Class 2-6-2T No. 4542 in the Yard awaiting inspection and a decision as to her fate. These locomotives were designed by Churchward in 1906 for light branch line use and were a development from the 4400 Class, with larger wheels.

3150 Class 2-6-2T No. 3171 on the 'Dump' in August 1957 awaiting her turn for the cutting-up torches. This was a Churchward design of 1906, subsequently fitted with superheater.

The first of the 3100 Class 2-6-2Ts in the Works yard. A Collett re-build of the 5310 Class, the five engines so treated had the pressure increased from 200lb per sq.in to 225lb and with the driving wheels reduced from 5ft 8in to 5ft 3in this resulted in a tractive effort increase from 25,670lb to 31,170lb. The design was introduced in 1938.

With indicator shelter removed but still without smoke deflectors, No. 71000 *Duke of Gloucester* looks out from the 'Barn' on to a variety of chimneys, only a few of which seem to bear the GWR capuchon.

Class 8P Pacific No. 71000 *Duke of Gloucester* was a frequent visitor to Swindon orks where a number of attempts were made to find the causes of the locomotive's or steaming qualities. Here No. 71000 is fitted with an indicator shelter for further ls.

Little more remains than the boiler and smokebox of ex-Burry Port & Gwendraeth Valley Railway 0-6-0T No. 2162, seen on a low-loader on the 'Dump' in April 1955.

Overleaf 'Castle' Class 4-6-0 No. 5019 *Treago Castle* in the course of a major overhaul inside the Works in October 1954. These locomotives were a Collett design of 1923 developed from Churchward's earlier 'Star' Class, an example of which is on page 64.

9000 Class 'Dukedog' No. 9020 in the process of being scrapped inside the Cutting-up Shop in August 1957. The nickname for this class of 4-4-0s was derived from the fact that the locomotives were 1936 rebuilds by Collett incorporating 'Duke' type boilers and 'Bulldog' frames.

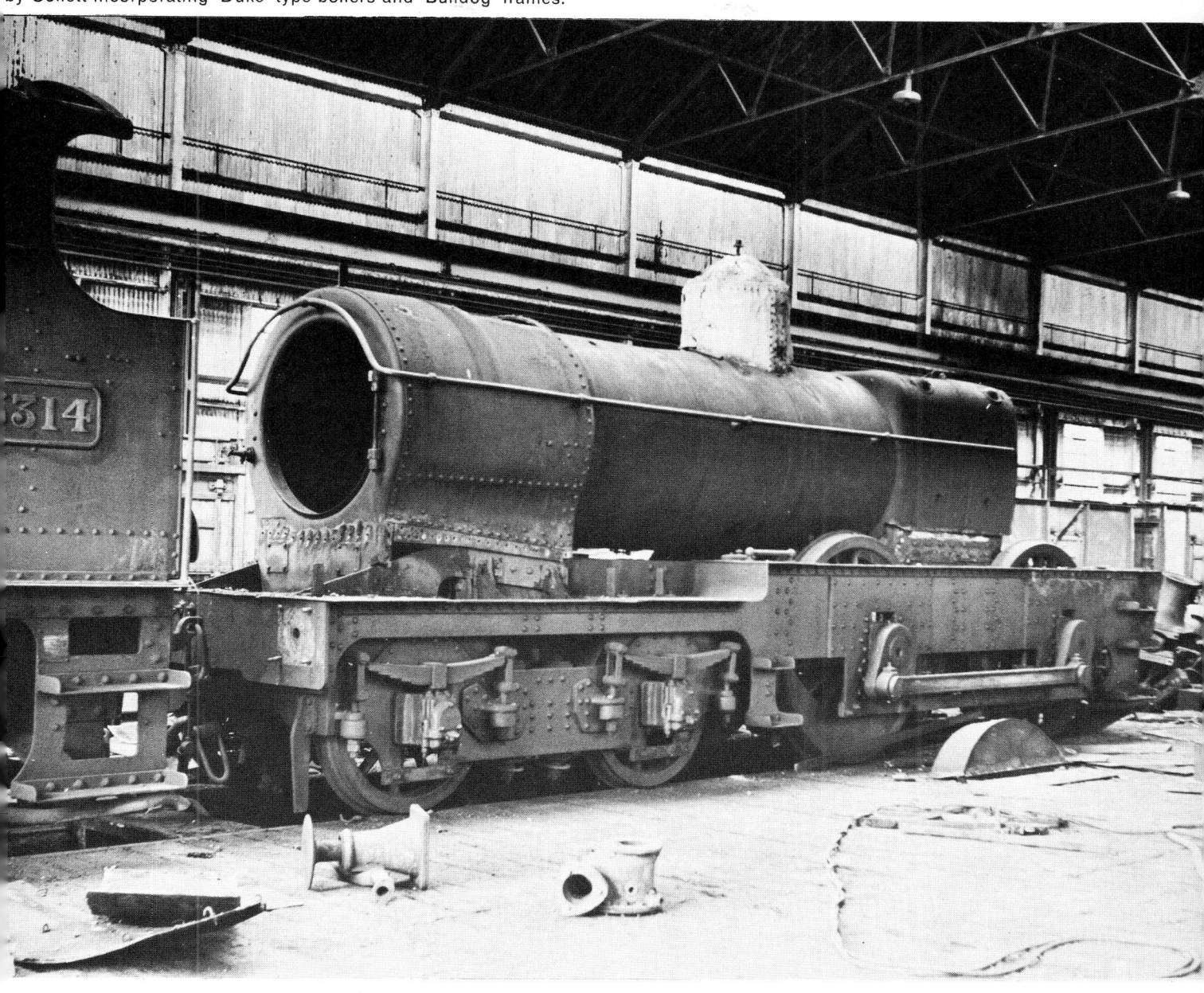

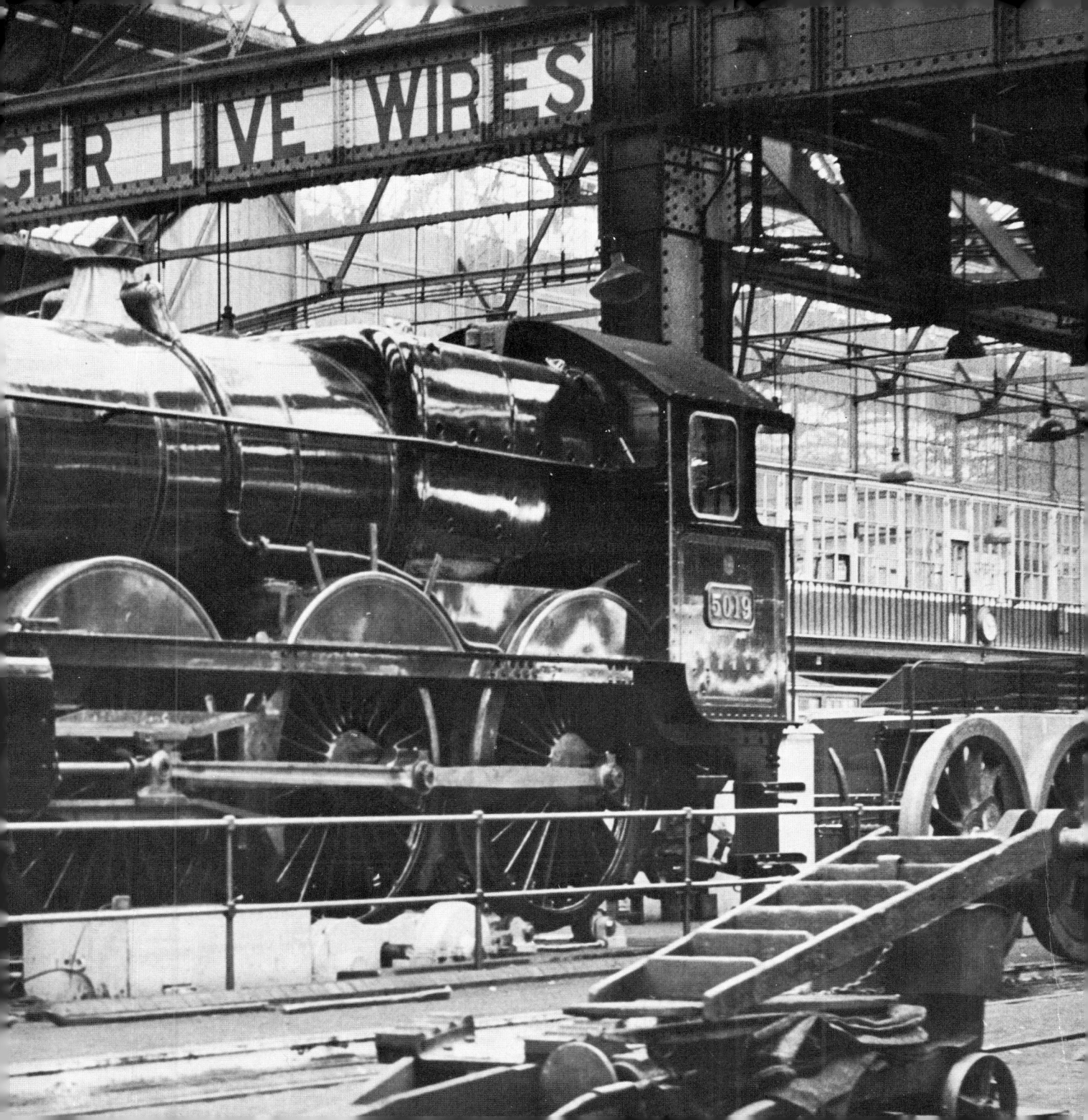

The nameplate of 'King' Class No. 6010

The nameplate of 'Castle' Class No. 7017

The nameplate of 'Star' Class No. 4049

The nameplate of 'Modified' Hall No. 6959

7200 Class 2-8-2T No. 7234 in the Works Yard after overhaul and repaint in November 1955. These engines were a rebuild by Collett in 1934 of Churchward's 1910-designed 4200 Class 2-8-0Ts, to increase coal and water capacity for main line working. No. 7234 was one of the straight framed series.

'Manor' Class 4-6-0 No. 7811 *Dunley Manor* fresh from shops in June 1955. Thirty of the class were built from 1938 to Collett's design for secondary line duty and incorporated some parts from withdrawn 4300 Class 2-6-0s.

Ex-Taff Vale Railway 'O4' Class 0-6-2T No. 279 in the Works yard, February 1955. The class was designed by Hurry Riches in 1907 and rebuilt by the GWR with a superheated taper boiler from 1924.

Midland & South Western Junction Railway 2-4-0 No. 1336 on the 'Dump' in May 1953. ...signed for the railway by Dübs in 1894, the three engines in this class were re-boilered ...the GWR some thirty years later. They finished their days in the Reading district ...ere they could often be seen on the Lambourne Valley line. [A. R. Carpenter]

2181 Class 0-6-0PT No. 2186 soaks up the sun for the last time before entering the Cutting-up Shop from the 'Dump' in Spring 1955. Originally a Dean saddle tank, this engine was first rebuilt with pannier tanks and classed '2021', then in 1939 it was modified again with increased braking power for work on heavy gradients and given the final '2181' classification.

1366 Class 0-6-0PT No. 1369 in use as Works shunter. The six engines in this class were a Collett 1934 development of Churchward's 1361 Class 0-6-0ST, an example of which is shown on page 35.

Ex-Burry Port & Gwendraeth Valley Railway 0-6-PT No. 2176, minus connecting rods and number plate, awaiting the cutting torch on the 'Dump'. This was an Avonside design of 1907 rebuilt by the GWR. Someone has hopefully chalked 'To Cardiff Museum' on the side of the saddle tank but, unfortunately, No. 2176 was never preserved.

1361 Class 0-6-0ST No. 1365 acting as Swindon station pilot after overhaul in the works in April 1955. The five locomotives in this class were designed by Churchward in 1910 for use as dock shunters.

x-Taff Vale 0-6-2T No. 337, having arrived at the Works from Radyr, awaits its fate in September 1954. lthough similar in appearance to the other Taff Vale 'A' Class, illustrated on page 10, this example differed having a lower boiler pressure, larger cylinders and lower tractive effort.

)21 Class 0-6-0PT No. 2082, minus connecting rods, in line for the Cutting-up Shop in June 1955. The class as designed by Dean in 1897 as saddle tanks but were subsequently rebuilt as panniers. This particular comotive spent its final years working at Birkenhead Docks.

Ex-Brecon & Merthyr Railway 0-6-2T No. 435 in use as a stationary boiler in the Works in the Autumn of 1954. A Dunbar 1915 design, the class was fitted with a taper boiler by the GWR in 1926.

No. 7001 *Sir James Milne*, one of the 'Castle' Class, resplendent in green livery, is watered up ready for the road again after a complete overhaul before returning to her home shed at Old Oak Common (81A).

7400 Class 0-6-0PT No. 7402, from Carmarthen (87G) shed, outside the Works in February 1955 after overhaul. This class was basically the same as the 6400 0-6-0PTs shown on page 58 but were not fitted for push and pull working. There were 50 engines in the class, which was introduced by Collett in 1936.

The Swiss-built Brown Boveri gas-turbine unit No. 18000 outside the Works in 1957 alongside a 2800 Class 2-8-0. 18000 was powered by four independently mounted motors with spring drive giving a rated horse-power of 2,500 and weighed 115 tons. Introduced in 1949, it was eventually sold abroad after spending a considerable amount of its life undergoing various tests and repairs.

BR Standard Class 4MT 4-6-0 No. 75073 in mint condition in the Works Yard in November 1955.

Standard Class 9F 2-10-0 No. 92005, from Newport (Ebbw Junct[ion]) shed, inside the Works in the Summer of 1957 awaiting repair follo[wing] accident damage.

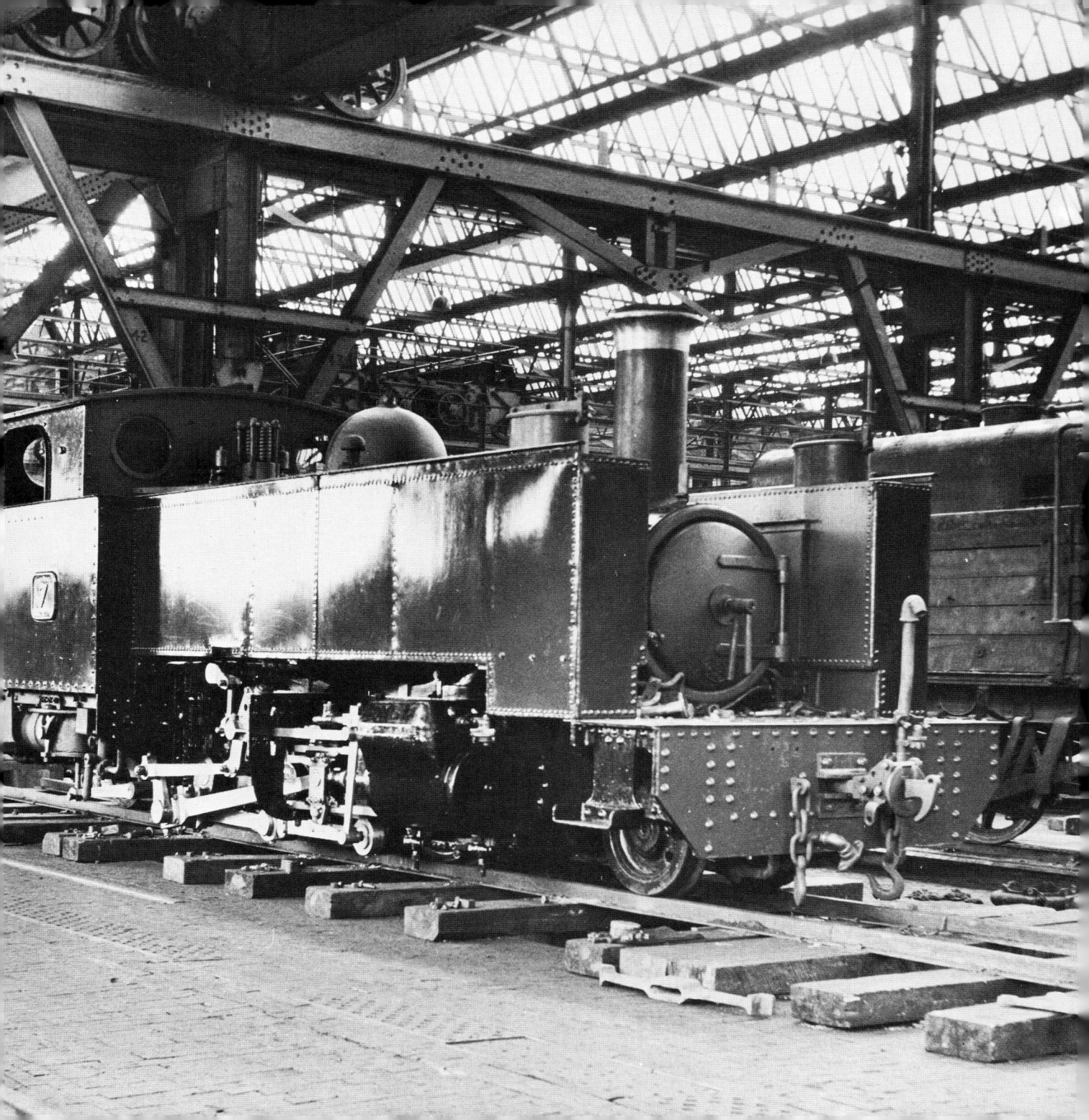

Vale of Rheidol No. 7, later to carry the name *Owain Glyndwr*, in the course of overhaul in the Works in 1955. This 1ft 11½in gauge 2-6-2T was a Davies & Metcalfe design of 1902 and is still in use on the Vale of Rheidol line from Aberystwyth to Devil's Bridge. Opposite, a close-up of the motion of No. 7, and (below) an example of the type of nameplate fitted by British Railways to No. 8 of the same class.

No. 6018 *King Henry VI* resplendent in the sunshine after a complete overhaul and re-paint in lined-out green. Introduced by Collett in 1927, most of the class, including No. 6018, were fitted with 4-row superheaters in 1947.

'Grange' Class No. 6831 *Bearley Grange*, bearing a 6C (Birkenhead) shed plate, outside the Stock Shed, after a minor overhaul and with the front end re-painted. The 80 locomotives of this class were designed by Collett and introduced from 1936, a variation of the 'Halls' with smaller wheels. Like the 'Manors', they incorporated some parts from withdrawn 4300 Class 2-6-0s.

'Hall' Class 4-6-0 No. 6950 *Kingsthorpe Hall*, acting as Works shunter, heads two 3800 Class 2-8-0s, a 2800 Class 2-8-0 and a WD 2-8-0 away from the Works alongside the main line in April 1955. All five locomotives were in steam.

5400 Class 0-6-0PT No. 5403, from Westbury shed, inside the Works in November 1955 awaiting attention. The 25 engines of the class were a Collett design dating from 1931 and were push and pull fitted. They were a familiar sight in the London area particularly, working most of the auto trains around the capital for many years.

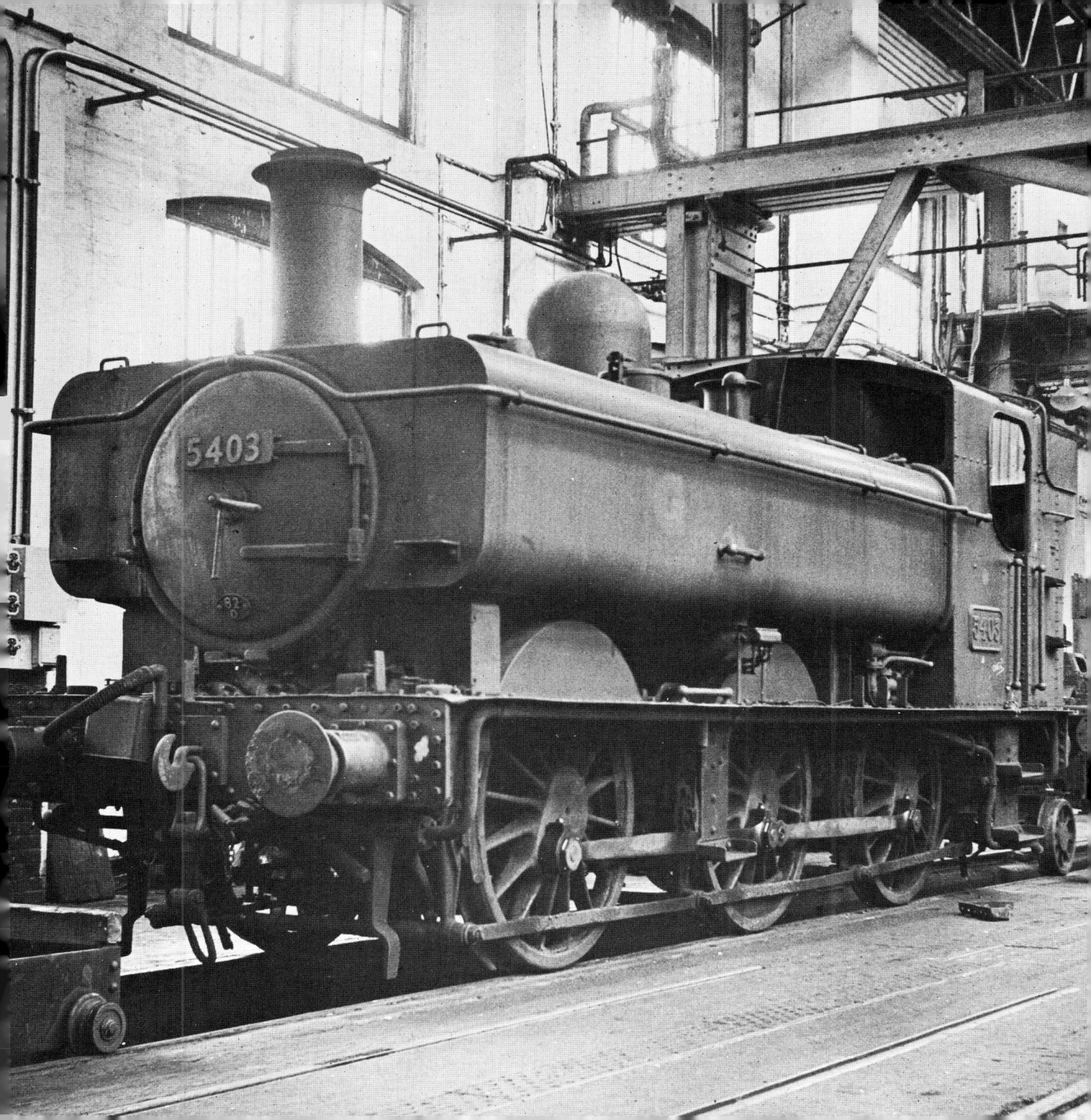

'County' Class 4-6-0 No. 1028 *County of Warwick*, from Bristol (Bath Road), had to be taken off a Bristol to Paddington express with axle trouble and here awaits clearance to enter Swindon Works for attention.

Swindon Works saw strangers from time to time such as modified 'Merchant Nav Pacific No. 35025 *Brocklebank Line* inside 'The Barn' in August 1957 during the period th data on the design was being obtained on the Testing Plant.

Ex-Alexandra (Newport & South Wales) Docks & Railway 0-6-0T No. 666, lacking its centre pair of wheels and connecting rods, awaiting final cutting-up in 1955. This sturdy little engine was a Kerr Stuart design of World War I for the Railway Operating Division and was purchased by the Alexandra Docks Co in 1919.

One of the tiny Departmental four-coupled petrol locomotives DER 26 awaits cutting up on the Triangle in the Winter of 1955.

Three old locomotives on the Swindon Dump awaiting their turn under the cutting torch; ex-Taff Vale 0-6-2T No. 309, Dean 2181 Class 0-6-0PT No. 2186 and ex-Burry Port & Gwendraeth Valley 0-6-0ST No. 2176.

2-8-0 No. 2836 of the 2800 Class in 'ex-Works' condition poses in the Yard in 1957. 100 of these engines were built to Churchward's design and another 67 with side windows to the cabs and some detail alterations were added in 1938—under Collett's regime.

'Castle' Class No. 5000 *Launceston Castle*, looking immaculate after being repainted, posed for a Swindon Open Day in 1956.

With nameplates, shed plates and cab numbers all removed three 'King' 4-6-0s and a 5101 Class 2-6-2T await their fate outside the Works in 1963. [P. J. Lynch]

6400 Class 0-6-0PT No. 6405, from Croes Newydd shed, awaits attention on the Triangle. These panniers were designed by Collett and introduced in 1932 for light passenger work, being fitted for push and pull use.

One of the 1101 Class 0-4-0Ts awaiting Works attention in April 1957. The six locomotives in this class were designed and constructed by Avonsides to GWR requirements in 1926 and were designated as dock shunters.

'County' Class No. 1015 *County of Gloucester* undergoing a major overhaul in the shops late in 1954.

First of the BR Standard Class 9Fs, No. 92000, allocated to Ebbw Junction shed (86A), awaiting attention inside 'A' Shop. A Riddles design, these very successful locomotives eventually numbered over 200 and two have been preserved.

2800 Class 2-8-0 No. 2841, stands outside the Works in November 1955 before being returned to her home shed at Oxley (84B).

Ex-Cardiff Railway 0-4-0ST No. 1338 awaits attention inside the shed. Built by Kitson in 1898 this diminutive engine is still in existence having been obtained by the Somerset Railway Museum for its collection at Bleadon & Uphill Station.

1901 Class 0-6-0PT No.1991 after arrival at Swindon in the Spring of 1955 for cutting up. These locomotives were built as saddle tanks at Wolverhampton in the 1880's and, surprisingly, over forty of them survived into BR days.

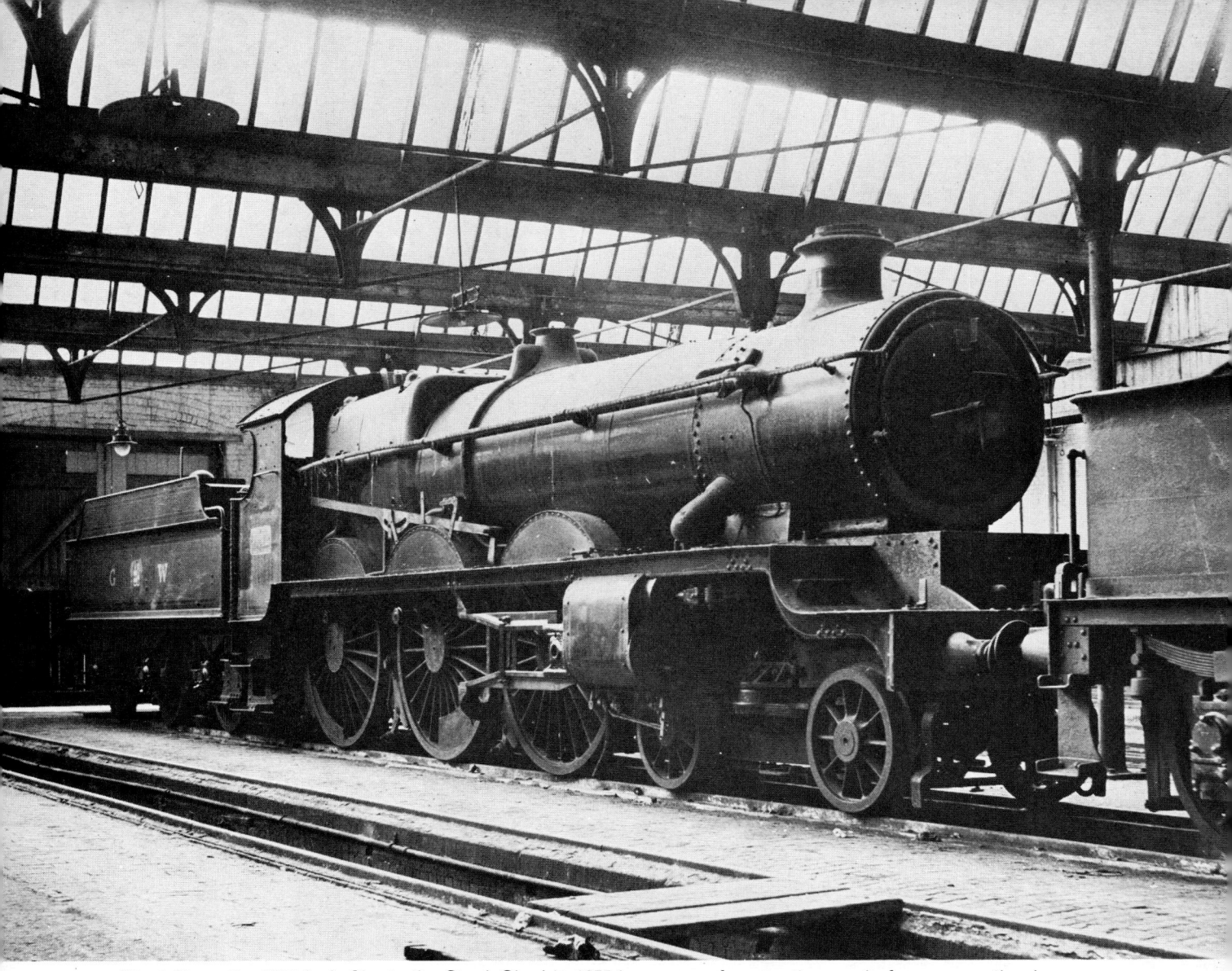

'Star' Class No. 4003 *Lode Star* in the Stock Shed in 1955 in course of renovation ready for preservation in Swindon Museum. Introduced by Churchward in 1907, this was the fine design that was the forerunner of the Collett 'Castles' and 'Kings'.

The sad remains of a 2021 Class pannier tank at one side of the Cutting-up Shop in 1955.

0-6-0PT No. 9400, first of the class, outside the Motive Power Depot. This engine was allocated to Swindon (82C) and despite being built a few months prior to Nationalisation still carries the letters 'GW' on the side nearly eight years later. Over 200 of these engines were eventually constructed, to Hawksworth's design.

Ex-Taff Vale 04 Class 0-6-2T No. 210 in an ominous queue of locomotives stretching from the Works Yard to the Cutting-up Shop. The re-boilering of this class by the GWR in 1924 prolonged their life by quite a few decades.

4575 Class 2-6-2T No. 5518 outside the Reception Shed after completion of a minor overhaul in 1954. These locomotives were introduced in 1927 and apart from the larger side tanks, greater weight and a few detail differences were identical to Churchward's 1906 4500 Class.

[Tw]o 5700 Class 0-6-0PTs Nos. 9700 and 8711 being overhauled in 'A' Shop in 1956. Introduced in 1929 by [Co]llett the class was a development of the 2021 pannier and eventually totalled 863. No. 9700 has a later [st]yle cab plus deeper tanks and condensing gear, having been built in 1933 for working the London Trans[po]rt Metropolitan line.

Swindon was accorded the honour of building British Railways' last steam locomotive, a Standard Class 9F No. 92220 subsequently named *Evening Star*. An earlier example of the class is shown here under construction in the Erecting Shop in 1958.

5101 Class 2-6-2T No. 4133, having emerged from the Works looking like new, awaits return to Westbury shed (82D) and a resumption of duties. These locomotives were introduced by Collett in 1929 and were a modification of his 5100 Class which, in turn, were based upon Churchward's original 3100 Class.

1500 Class 0-6-0PT No.1508 awaits attention outside the Works. Ten of these outside cylindered short wheel-base pannier tanks were built to Hawksworth's design in 1949 and while most of them were used from Old Oak Common for empty stock working in and out of Paddington, this particular example was allocated to Severn Tunnel Junction (86E).

On a Winter morning in 1955 two locomotives taken over by the GWR at the grouping await a decision as to their fate—ex-Taff Vale 0-6-2T No. 373 and ex-Cardiff Railway 0-6-0PT No. 683.

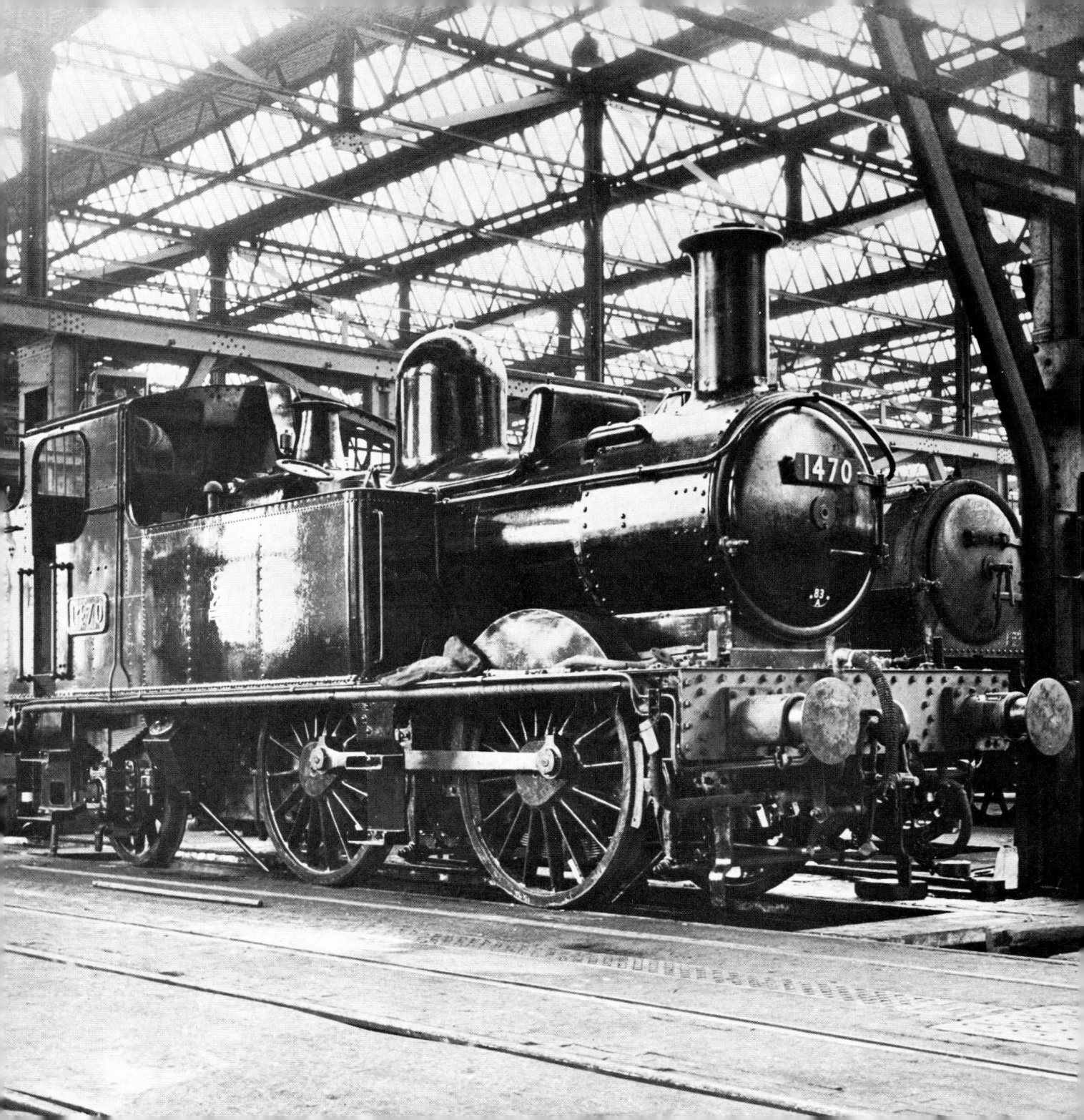

5800 Class 0-4-2T No. 5802 stands in the Works Yard in June 1955 still displaying 'G W' on the tank sides despite being overhauled and having a partial re-paint. It was perhaps not entirely coincidence that, like the locomotive depicted on page 67, this was also allocated to Swindon! The twenty locomotives in the 5800 Class were introduced by Collett in 1933, identical to the 1400s shown opposite, except that they were not fitted for push-and-pull working.

An immaculate little 1400 Class 0-4-2T No. 1470 stands in the Erecting Shop awaiting the final touches to a complete overhaul and re-paint before being returned to Newton Abbot (83A).

Worcester-based 5700 Class 0-6-0PT No. 3775 waits to return home after having been through the Works for a major overhaul.

A Collett 5100 Class 2-6-2T on the scrap line in November 1955. The class was introduced by Collett in 1928 as rebuilds of the original Churchward 3100s with increased weight and were subsequently fitted with superheaters.

2021 Class 0-6-0PT No. 2144, fitted with a spark arrester, awaiting scrapping.

The nameplate of 'Grange' Class No. 6835

The nameplate of 'Manor' Class No. 7819

The nameplate of 'City' Class No. 3440

The nameplate of 'County' Class No. 1017

Two scenes inside the Cutting-up Shop. On the left, 2-6-2T No. 4406, last of the class of eleven engines introduced in 1904 as a smaller version of the 4500 Class. An example of the latter is seen above, alongside an old Burry Port & Gwendraeth Valley saddle tank. These two were numbers 4534 and 2165 respectively.

Re-boilered ex-Rhymney 0-6-2T No. 44 on the 'Dump' in 1956 alongside 2021 Class 0-6-0PT No. 2072.

A passing cloud gives the impression that 0-6-0ST No. 2195 is in steam but, in fact, she was never to steam again. An ex-Burry Port & Gwendraeth Valley locomotive built in 1903, it is shown here on the scrap line in August 1953.
[A. R. Carpenter]

Two more locomotives in 'ex-Works' condition; above No. 5961 *Toynbee Hall*, in black and (below) No. 5025 *Chirk Castle* lined out in green. The 'Hall' was from Llanelly (82F) shed and the 'Castle' from Bristol Bath Road (82A).

Beautifully turned out and ready to return to normal duty as Swindon Works shunter, 1366 Class 0-6-0PT No. 1369 in a corner of the Works buildings.

5400 Class 0-6-0PT No. 5402, ready for the road again after overhaul and painting, alongside the wall of the main works building.

Ex-Swansea Harbour Trust 0-4-0ST No. 1142 on the Dump near the Works. This was the most powerful of the SHT tanks taken into GWR stock and was a Hudswell Clarke design introduced in 1911.

The vast size of the Erecting Shop is shown to advantage in this view photographed in the early 1960's. [Lawrence Waters]

2800 Class 2-8-0 No. 3822 awaiting Works attention. Eighty-four of these engines were built to Churchward's specifications between 1903 and 1919; Collett built a further 82 with side window cabs with only detail differences, between 1938 and 1942, of which No. 3822 was one—a real tribute to the quality of the original design.

Another 'Dukedog', No. 9010, in the yard on the same day, awaiting the same fate.

9000 Class 'Dukedog' 4-4-0 No. 9027, with top feed, heads a line of the class on the Triangle awaiting entry into the Cutting-up Shop in August 1957.

5600 Class 0-6-2T No. 5668, from Treherbert, outside the shed. Two hundred of the class were constructed to Collett's design between 1924 and 1928 and were intended primarily for use in South Wales, replacing the older locomotives of the absorbed companies.

Just out of Shops, 4300 Class 2-6-0 No. 5328, a Shrewsbury (84G) based locomotive, awaits the opportunity to return home. This class was designed by Churchward and introduced in 1911.

A rebuilt Dean Class 2021 0-6-0PT No. 2090 on the scrap line having been condemned after 52 years useful work.

The last three pannier tanks to be constructed, 1600 Class Nos. 1667, 1668 and 1669, near completion in the Erecting Shop in April 1955. A Hawksworth design, this class replaced older and similar engines throughout Western Region from 1949 onwards.

Nameplate of the last 'Castle' Class 4-6-0 to be built, No. 7037, unveiled by HRH Princess Elizabeth, Swindon Works on 15 November 1950.